CONFLUENCE

Confluence

Geoff Wilkinson

LOST VALLEY PRESS
HARDWICK, MA

ISBN: 978-1-935874-45-4

book designed by Sarah Bennett
shbennettbookdesign.com

front cover art by AJ Juarez

to Sally

TABLE OF CONTENTS

STREAMS

WAVES

We who believe in freedom
cannot rest.

Bernice Johnson Reagon, "Ella's Song"

From Water We Come

Birth Day

From salt and water we come.
Primordial slime and blood offer testimony.
We come from water and passion.
We struggle forth to breathe of our own accord.
We come from passion and hope,
Carried in our genes, gifts from our parents,
From theirs and theirs and theirs before.
We come from hope and starlight,
Shining through tears, through oceans
As the universe explodes.
We come from starlight, from timeless love,
To kick, to cry, to suck, to grip,
Even as this life we seek has its time.
We come from love and courage,
To seek our meaning,
To know and make our time.

Mother's Hands

Those are your grandmother's hands,
Mother, where did you find them?
Thick blue veins raised like a delta river
Winding through decades of family landscape.

Those are your mother's hands,
Mother, where did they find you?
Working, like hers, through the autumn years
Steadily tuned to the promise of spring.

Gift of Life

Song on the breeze
At light of dawn,
A tide of hope
To sail upon.

Soft golden throat,
New chance, a spark,
Sweet morning gift,
The meadow lark.

Spring Thing

Spring thing,
Purple wisdom heart,
Green field fertile,
Blue passion burning,
Lilac lover,
Steady pulse
In our awakening.

Large Animals

Large animals,
We arise quietly in the night,
Stir the grasses of our bedsheets,
Reposition and settle
Into disturbed dreams of the hunt.

Glitter Speck

A speck of glitter
Stuck to the side of her shoe,
Sparkling in fluorescent light,
Transports me from an endless meeting
To a night calmed beach—
Gazing at a brilliant star
Piercing the inky endlessness,
Reminding we stand on sand,
Great ocean of time lapping
Gently at our feet—
One tiny point,
One twinkling moment,
A life on her shoe.

Change of Tide

Empty rooms greet our return
Beds made, tucked sheets crisp
Where sons should be sleeping.
We watched waves crashing,
Shared memories as the moon tugged heartstrings
And tipped the ocean out of its bowl—
Foaming brine spilling over the beach lip
Washing away footprints and sand castles.

Sometimes When I'm Dead

Sometimes when I'm dead inside,
Feeling glum and mean,
I need to go regain my stride,
On a trail of rock and green,
Shadow dappled with the sun,
Streaming in through trees.

Murphy Point

The eagle's view pleases me,
Soaring on wings of exhalation,
Gazing over the expanse of wilderness below,
Hunting for inspiration.

Impressions

Here are lizard tracks and desert rat,
Boot prints of hikers,
Tiny impressions and large,
Catching first light, creating
Shadows of visibility
In smooth sand.
We make our ways together
Up and down the hill,
Among snakeweed and yucca,
Foraging one and all.
Some seek food,
Some the nourishment of stillness
In the swallow's call, the fresh morning breeze,
The haunting beauty of landscape
Shaped by water, wind, and uncountable dawns.

High Hut

Before the birds sing,
Coral wafts over the obsidian curve of South Twin,
Here and there, diamonds settle
As earth turns toward morning.
Before spruce emerges from darkness,
Before goldenrod waves in the breeze,
Before pine marten furtively forages,
Before human cares and carnage,
Time inhales as cook lights the range
Ahead of the sun.

Preposterous Moderation

Acrylics and watercolors,
Partially used,
Possibly hardened in crumpled tubes,
Remnants of bottles of single malt Scotch,
Savored and carefully parsed over years—
Some things I use
In preposterous moderation.
No need to replace what
One hasn't consumed.
How is it then
That time, so precious,
Pours freely
Through the open chutes of my days?

Quabbin

I bring water to the source of water,
After sixty trips around the sun.
I carry a staff of beaver wood,
I enter the water, become the water,
Become the gliding hawk, the singing tanager.
I walk the old road,
With vernal pools and fiddlehead ferns,
Past stone walls laid before the dams were built,
Before towns were submerged to fill the valley.
I come west to find the source of water,
After sixty trips around the sun,
Return east to drink the water,
As I start another one.

Mourning Paper

My beloved sleeps,
Breath rising and falling like aspirations.
Outside, the pines are strangely still,
Despite a gathering storm.
Daffodils bloom, mating season is upon us.
A robin devours a helpless worm,
Then jumps and whirls about, alert to attack.
A train whistle breaks the silence.
Veterans pile higher in refrigerator trucks.
Hands press from both sides of nursing home windows.
Magnates pull heartstrings and pick pockets.
Whether the dawn comes gray or golden,
Each day begins the same:
A surging tally of infection and death
Waits on our doorstep.

Empty Houses

Death lurks and prances here
Like a fat, stupid turkey shimmering
In the afternoon sun, strutting about,
Pecking bugs in the dirt amidst
Daffodils and green leaves of tulips
Emerging despite the drought
Our long, dry winter left behind.

The mantle clock ticks,
Because we disabled its chime.
We need no reminder.
We already have trembling hands, fading memories,
Failing hearts, emptying houses, and
Photos of yesteryear displayed on the pages
Of newspaper sections we used to ignore.

Resolution

We walked festering afterwards,
Pumpkin light bleeding into leaden clouds.
You said I could bathe unmolested
In flaming poison ivy.
I pretended you were at fault
For the silence that echoed our labored breathing.
But we confessed apologies later,
Three candles flickering,
As you split my pomegranate soul, tenderly
Extracting flinty little seeds and spilling
Sweet juices of agony.

Metronome

In the tangle of limbs
Under our covers,
We were face to face
As I awoke.
A wisp of your hair
Fell curving between us
Across your cheek.
Forced right by your exhaled breath
(Or was it mine?)
It sprang back into place
As you breathed in
(Or was it me?)
I held my breath to find out
It was you
Moving that metronome
of silver gossamer
Back and forth
In the sweet warm musk
We breathed together
In borrowed moments
Tender and precious
As you slept.

Valentine

Tomato vulva
Mother's lipstick
Couch you wanted
Silken robe
Cotton candy
Cherry pie
Turning seasons
Spinning globe
Castle Desert Virgin Block
Moonlit ocean, breaking dawn
Pomegranate children gone
Roses, blood, Burgundy
Strawberry licorice, raspberry
Ruby earring, nipple, tongue
Burning sunsets, laughing eyes
Electric fingers, velvet thighs
Music breathing, kissing me
Building, bursting, letting go
Luscious, damp, amazing, slow
Rising, stretching, supple, fine
Yours forever, ever mine
Thankful for you,
Valentine.

Mother's Day

Young men with dreams and visions of their own
Who work and study far from where they played
From loving seed to budding trees have grown
With branches spreading wide, though roots have stayed.
Once fragile babes whose grips and sucks were strong
Who gazed into their mother's loving eyes
Through tender days and trying nights so long
Still constantly amaze and give surprise.
A windy morn moves shadows on our sill
Leaves dancing in the sun as if to sing
Life's music with true voice and steady will
A timeless praise for wondrous mothering.
        No man has lived with greater gratitude
        Than I, for sharing parenthood with you.

Jazz Drummer

You did your duty
Twenty minutes at a time,
Making progress
But missing the rhyme,
While your brother escaped in orgies of notes,
Oblivious to the clock
Until we dragged him smiling
To the dinner table.

How long did it take us
To wake up and hear the music,
Trapped and leaking from
Tapping toes and drumming fingers,
Aching for release with two limbs wasted
While you served hard time,
Carefully pressing keys
Your father longed to master?

Now there's nowhere on this green blue planet
Where insects quiver and nations quake
And bodies move for pleasure's sake
Where you can't join souls
With perfect strangers,
Sticks flying, limits dying,
Playing with time, soaring on wings
Of the universal tongue.

Anniversary

When fire has claimed the land,
All that it can,
When dams are belatedly destroyed,
Rivers drained and fish depleted,
Even then, at dawn, earth's orchestra will stir.
Music will rise as the shameless eastern sky parades its glory.
Wind will rustle leaves,
Newborn babes will cry for the departed,
The cardinal will call,
The mourning dove will answer.
After the final breath is taken, whale song, mystery,
Life dancing in memory's arms,
Love unbound from time.

You connect us all like aspen roots on a golden hillside,
Each rippling fin and rustling feather.
You, the glow of a conch shell illuminated by morning sun,
The space between the letters of all the words
In every book imagined,
You, a chord sounding after the bell is still,
Who claims the broken spirit and nourishes.
You, with laughing eyes and tingling tongue,
Who goes about the business of caring
Without care or calculation, like the sun and the tides,
A monarch wing unfolding, a river of raindrops mixed
    with tears,
The heart of the holy living in and through you, holding me.

Water is Body

You say we carry the river, its body of water, in our body.
Body and water are the same. Water is body, energy,
    medicine, prayer.
I am the water flowing in the river, yes, and the ocean and
    the stream,

The nectar on the hummingbird's tongue, the breaking water
    of birth,
Tears flowing down my lover's cheeks as she grieves
All the deaths that have crashed upon her shore.

I am the gurgling forest brook, ageless reminder that
Time is not real; death is for the living,
The falling, parted, open, endless water.

I am urine flowing unbidden into mother's chair cushion,
As she reminisces about wading in the creeks of
    her childhood,
Where woodland fairies said she would be safe.

I am the water missing from barren farmland,
The cleansing rain and flooding torrent,
The sacred water of new life and impending passage.

I am the water leaking through a rented roof, corroding walls
Where cabinets sag and roaches nest.
I am spittle in the tyrant's fulmination,

Poison flowing in a grade school fountain,
Water rising as mist from a still dawn pond,
Reflecting sentinel pines, inviting the naked to enter.

I fill thirsty dancers and rip babies from loving arms,
Carrying us downstream into the mysteries of stardust
    and souls,
Where we are all the water, all sisters and brothers, one body,
    all one.

Ripples
(Haiku)

Surfacing

Swimming in the sea,
Stroke after wonderful stroke,
Rocking in the womb.

Shooting star dazzles
Beauty writ upon the sky
Insensible death.

Enjoy these moments
Passing rapidly as dreams
Children leave too soon.

All of these years now,
And still I rise rock solid
To your softest touch.

Suddenly you popped,
Sweet magnolia blossom,
Opened with kisses.

Glistening in the trees
An ocean of colored gems,
Sun-washed snow raining.

Certain catalyst
Fosters collaboration:
The promise of cash.

Who will know or care
What harried these commuters
In a hundred years?

Erratics

This pond must surely
Be a special private place
For legions of us.

Campfire glows like
Pyres in Varanasi,
Restoring our souls.

Wildly flailing towel,
Defense against the dark arts,
Horse flies attacking.

Get back on the bike
Peddle and listen to jazz
Take pain with pleasure.

Swaying on my feet,
An old cartoon character,
Stone in love with you.

Into the wider world
Launched from your perfect belly,
Our boys Sally forth.

Reading the death toll
With snow falling in April,
Will spring ever come?

Falling leaves in June
Should not be happening here,
Nor these school shootings.

Contemplation

Retirement looms
Like end of adolescence.
Too many questions

For the little mouse,
Regarding a cheese mountain,
Unsure where to start.

Possibilities
Swirl like perpetual fog
Blanketing old spruce.

You cannot eat it
All at once anyway, mouse.
Just take the first bite

The path will open
Like morning sun burning through,
Revealing the sea.

 Layers

Confluence Overlook

I walk through a haunted valley
Of sentinel needles.
Ancients surround me,
Their faces clear in glowing sandstone,
Profiles chiseled in burgundy shale,
Voices carrying over slick rock
That never dies,
Just crumbles to give life
To sage and juniper,
Indigo columbine, waving fields of grass.
Beyond this precipice where the trail ends,
Where a dream beckons,
A staring lizard knows heaven's conceit:
Life is shared in time
Where the rivers meet.

Polished Rocks

Hopes and hurts cascade
Over the polished rocks of our friendship,
Swirling, leaping, moving downstream,
Catching, circling in back water eddies
Of doubt cradled in moss covered banks,
Sharp branches piercing through mirrored surfaces
Into the depths where days pass into years,
Where children grow and bodies soften,
Where transgressions are forgiven
After the conversation resumes,
Where the stream reclaims our momentum,
Carrying truth and nonsense together
Toward the sea.

Cottonwoods

There is always a creek, a wash,
A slow moving silver ribbon
Threading through the canyon floor
Where Ancient Ones
Gaze from their ruins.
Cottonwoods crowd along the banks,
Luscious, cool, pernicious marauders,
Sucking dry the source of life
For corn, squash, and fruit trees.
I tell Benjamin my grandfather had a cottonwood
And called it a dirty tree.
We laugh together, both grandfathers now.
He welcomes the park service work crews
And youth volunteer corps,
Chopping and burning the cottonwoods.
He hopes the water table will rise again
So he can restore his great grandmother's field.
Meanwhile, the cottonwoods send forth
Their springtime blizzard of seeds,
Sailing the breeze and simmering in the sun.
Did they arrive by the hands of man
Or the wings of birds?
Are they invaders or inheritors?
Benjamin would be too polite to scoff
At such inanity.

Of course, we shape the world to our needs.
We chop cottonwoods to plant
We extract rare earth to manufacture
We breathe agrarian in, digital out.
We seek balance and fortune
While the seeds fly.

Mustangs

I need help identifying the mustangs
Among dozens of horses
Grazing as the sun settles behind Tuyuna Mesa.
Two ranch hands, in separate encounters,
Give different information about
The same three animals.
These two, says one,
Have some mustang in them,
But this one is the real thing.
This one, says the other, is a poor excuse
For a mustang,
But these two are the real deal.
I trust him because the sun has leathered
His neck and whiskered face,
Because of the blurred tattoos on
His wiry forearm,
Because of the way he looks at me.
He has sized me up, too.
We share enough in common,
From our different worlds,
That when he tells me
These two have never been ridden,
And probably never will be,
We both know we agree
That's the way it should be.

Daughter of the Prairie

She longs for breaking surf—
Sparkling serenity, rising as a wall of turquoise glass,
Tumbling into laughing foam,
Or rhythmic thunder, churning sand and stone,
Crashing mountains to mock the horizon line.
Either would be fine
For the daughter of the prairie,
Longing for a life she only might have known.
Ever learning, 'til learning turns aside,
We neither guide the wind,
Nor tame the tide.
White caps dance and disappear
Like her memories,
Into the depths of time,
As the sun embraces her,
And oceans sing,
We take you as you are, sublime.

Give Us This Day

They embrace on the pier at midnight,
Silhouetted in stern lights,
Resolute, fears packed tight as the gear in his duffle.
The moon watches from behind careening clouds,
Unsentimental as the tossing charcoal sea,
Witness to a final kiss, a reminder, a good luck wish,
A promise he has no power to keep.
The tail lights of her pick-up vanish into town
As the boat recedes into ink and wind,
A speck of light,
Hope and history balanced
On an invisible horizon.

125th Street Station

He shoots and misses
In the shadow of a brick tower,
Moves swiftly to the rebound
Puts it up again,
As our train pulls into 125th Street Station.
Rusting security grates cover windows,
Pillows bulge from broken panes.
His shirt striped red, yellow, blue,
His jeans brand new,
His next shot sails true.

Troubles

Delfred knows whose life is marked
By the white cross with plastic flowers
At the side of the canyon road.
It was his cousin.
It happens, he says,
As if driving off the road was
Part of the natural order.
Delfred needs a ride to his uncle's ranch
Up near Spider Rock because
His girlfriend is mad at him.
She refused to pick him up at the trailhead
After his overnight in the canyon valley.
I went down to take care of my grandmother's sheep,
    he says,
But she thinks I went down to meet another girl.
We've been together five years, he says,
Blue bandana draped over thick black hair,
But we have our troubles.
Delfred declines an offer of trail mix
In favor of more water.
His thirst runs deep.
It happens.

Esteemed Friend

He wields his praise like a rapier,
Deftly lavishing affection and affirmation,
For favor's gain, for acquiescence,
The consummate seducer.
He wears his sacrifice like elegant silk,
Our humble servant leader, bow-tied benefactor,
Quick to parry any hint of infidelity
With the threat of banishment.

Blueberry Pickers

Black bodies stoop
In green fields
Under yellow sun
Where gulls soar
And tides run.
Black hands fly
Picking sweet berries
For white tables
With tennis courts
And shingled gables.
Black songs echo
Where green crabs
Crawl in gray mud
And wine flows
Like precious blood.

Group Home

Sitting on a porch step,
Blinking in the morning sun,
Cigarette smoldering in your relaxed hand,
You watch my approach,
Quick paced briefcaser, hurrying for the train.
"How's Robin," you ask naturally,
As if we were old friends,
As if I knew who you were talking about,
As if you knew.
"Good," I reply pleasantly, "Good."
Perhaps this makes me Batman.
Perhaps I am the herald of Spring.
Your housemates sit behind you in shadow,
One rocking silently, one staring ahead,
Steeped in their own realities,
Minds easier to fathom than the
Convoluted passions of warmongers
And men who tweak laws to better plunder and pollute,
As if their daughters and sons, with ours,
Were spinning ahead into different histories,
As if we lived beneath different suns.

If It Bleeds

It has come to this—
The whole world watching
Me naked in the rain.
Down to this—
A news portrait of misery
Defiant in my pain.
Flood waters rise
As they sip morning coffee
Muddy river swirls
where the street should be,
Belongings balanced on the stair
Cholera lurking in the back pages
I clutch what I can carry
Ignoring the photographer
I survey the chaos
Head held high
So all may see
My dignity.

Hibernian Hall

Babies lying dead in the street,
She said,
Like fish washed up on shore,
The wounded waiting without strength
To cry,
Hundreds by the thousands.
So we put our backs into it
As one,
Sorting all this clothing,
Imagining who used to wear
This skirt,
This shirt, this pair of pants,
Imagining who will open
This box,
Passed down a human chain
To waiting truck, then boat or plane.
Our hearts,
Full of the prayerful songs
They're singing, even in the face
Of death,
Even as the shouting
Stops from underneath the rubble,
Again.
Music coursing through our
Grunts and laughs, the fierce pace of our
Labor,

Done because we want to,
Knowing that community is
Power,
Desperate to help somehow.

Suicide

You came to me in a dream tonight,
Not wearing the noose you used,
But resurrected, cheerleader cellist in a white gown
Seen through a window, entering the party,
Claiming it had been a hoax,
You were with us still,
Triggering incredulous questions,
Unlike those that have tormented since,
Corrosive dripping of a faucet I might have closed,
The how and why and might have been,
Of your tortured departure,
Questions dissolving as I woke
With your ghost in the room,
Again, always, forever your ghost.

In the Mosque

I closed my eyes and sat legs folded
As your Muslim brothers prayed before us,
Standing, bowing, kneeling, prone,
Chanting as we waited for your service to begin.
I did not imagine the dirt on my shoes
Or blister under my wedding band
That would come later
After joining them in burying you.
My breath settled and I recalled
How I first understood
When we take our final breath
In and out, and then no more,
Only our loved ones will suffer.

Charioteer

You were Apollo,
Shaper of lives, maker of days.
You glowed golden,
Coaxing us from the earth,
Bathing and nourishing,
Ripening us in warmth.
You cast and banished shadows,
Burned us under stinging rays,
Soothed us in peach and copper afterglows.
We saw you reflected in silvery moonlight,
Dancing on dark waters.
You might have been the ocean for your depth,
Might have been the cosmos that you entered.
You might have pulled the tides,
But we revolved around you,
You, of the daylight,
Ravaged in twilight,
Extinguished like the final flutter
Of flame off a glowing ember.
Burning brightly still.

Light Becomes Her

Light becomes her,
The daffodil's illumination,
The peach glow of a summer dawn,
The pulse of an autumn fire,
The crystal of a winter morn.

Light infuses her poetry,
Softens her cheek,
Radiates the quiet passion of
Her clear thought and burning love.

How much beauty these eyes have beheld.
How much pain these hands have touched.
Who can know the fullness of this heart,
The depth of this wisdom?

We laugh in the light of her laughter,
Walk in her graceful footsteps,
Join in her celebration,
Share in her thanks.

Light becomes her,
The bold full moon,
The gaudy sunset,
The arching rainbow,
The guiding star.

Sister Talk

I see you gazing at my reflected light
Across the water you love so well,
Marveling to imagine you were once so full,

As you empty against your will,
Longing for the strength of one last swim
Into my essence.

We measure time differently but wane together,
You with windswept children
Rushing like waves to toss upon your shore,

Me, pulling the tides forever,
Longing for someone's touch,
Both of us loved from afar by too many to count.

You do us proud, nurturing to the end,
Sharing goodbyes others could not give,
Exhorting them to hold together,

Even as you loosen your hold
On the world of cares,
Moving with me toward the eternal horizon.

I also shine through trees, you know,
Illuminate snow-capped mountains,
Smile upon the sleeping doe and spilling brook.

I will cast soft light upon your tombstone,
With its perfect font and simple truth,
Through ages that will make a mockery of youth.

And you will join me finally,
Another point and ripple in my glow,
Forever loved and missed by those you know.

Peace Guide Your Journey

Peace guide your journey,
Light lead the way.
I would have kept you another day.
Would I could hold you in my arms,
Peace guide your journey,
Keep you from harm.

Through tears of love,
I bid you live
And profit by the strength you give.
Let prayers go forth upon this song:
Banish the pain you've fought so long.

Though from the full moon
Light is waning,
And from your body life does drain,
I love you only as you are.
The darker night reveals new stars.

Peace guide your journey,
Light lead the way.
I would have kept you another day.
Would I could hold you in my arms,
Peace guide your journey,
Keep you from harm.

Trilogy for Linda

I. Woodpecker

She likes the sound of the woodpecker
Breaking the stillness while the world wakes,
The sweet staccato exhalation,
Repeated yet unpredictable,
A touch of the wild, a familiar mystery,
The joy of discovery with every flurry,
Every call that might be answered,
Every path that might be traveled,
Every child welcomed, every tender kiss,
Every song upon the wind,
Until stillness accompanies flight
Like the sudden, unexpected departure of a beloved soul
Extinguishes light.

II. Catbird

We know this catbird,
Riffing through his impressive repertoire,
Pure throated emissary for the arriving spring,
Singing us awake earlier than we'd prefer,
Heralding the glory of life
As we lie with death on our minds.
He returns from worlds unknown,
But we cannot bring back the ones we love.

Sing on, friend.
It is better that we rise with you
Than molder in this bed.

III. Cardinal

We both saw it, a flash of crimson
As the sun settled through overcast skies into a flat, gray sea,
Incongruous, a celestial trick, another reminder,
Her soul ablaze, still aglow in clouds rolling east,
Reflected on wet cheeks,
Sitting stately among branches silhouetted against snow,
Riffling our senses, soothing, inciting,
Trying to convey the cardinal truth.

Agent Orange

In vivid dreams he returns from the dead
Fortifying parties with his infectious smile
Filling water balloons for laughing children

He drives jeeps for the general command
Filling water balloons for laughing children
Loads barrels of defoliant onto waiting planes

He casts perfectly above the rushing river
Loads barrels of defoliant onto waiting planes
Thrills to the tug of life captured on his line

He admires her entering his room
Thrills to the tug of life captured on his line
Makes her smile despite the blood count

He wires buildings for machines he doesn't use
Makes her smile despite the blood count
Hoists a purring cat to his shoulder

He complains about veggies and bitter herbal tea
Hoists a purring cat to his shoulder
Makes it to the waiting car leaning on a friend

He wastes away as the war finally takes him
Makes it to the waiting car leaning on a friend
Finally gets a boat of his own

He confounds time with her ferocious love
Finally gets a boat of his own
Slipping away on the early tide

He grins suspended in the photo frame
Slipping away on the early tide
Fortifying parties with his infectious smile.

Streams

Shelling

Desperados, raking the muck with a piece of driftwood,
Hoping to find buried treasure—
A murex, perhaps, or better yet

An unbroken tulip—
We search like insatiable children on Christmas morning
Eager for one more present beneath the tree,

Breathing in the sweet smell of dying creatures
Left behind on the tide,
Shoulder to knee with people who collect shells

In shopping bags, taking whatever they can
Because they can, like predatory lenders
Hungry for every last dollar,

Keeping even the inhabited ones,
Robbing the lives
As well as the homes.

Fires in the West

All the stars are Mars red,
And the cantaloupe moon whispers,
Fires in the West.
If beauty is the splendor of truth and
Beautiful that the apprehension of which pleases,
Who can celebrate these discolored heavens?
Bring back our diamonds for the gathering twilight!
Each generation grows to know what it misses,
But must study to learn what was already lost.
Who will recall geese flying south in formation?
Who will learn they went squawking by the thousands
Over crimson maples and towering firs,
Consumed now in flames?

Three Shots

The BVM is discovered yet again,
Majestic in the bark of a condemned tree,
Gazing upon men clubbed and moaning on their backs,
Knives drawn at exposed throats.
She sees insect hoards advancing,
Birds picking at immigrant corpses
Rotting in the desert sun.
She grasps the hideous math of inoculation:
Three shots for the rich against a mutating virus,
None for the poor of neglected continents.
She weeps without a cell phone.
Who to call?

Hungry Water

It happens in sleek elevators when the seabed buckles,
In shelters and shooting galleries,
Incubators and imaginations,
Lovers' arms and locked wards,
When the ocean throws back its head and roars,
Rising to reclaim what time has stolen,
Rushing upon the land, heedless and greedy,
Challenging the wind, bellowing across the plain,
Mocking lives and labors,
Carrying houses like bubbles on a poison brine.

It happens when the planet tips, balance shifts,
When children hang themselves, and
Wrinkled couples wake together as strangers.
It happens when a people rises up
Angry as the sea, demanding liberty,
As magma gurgles and the system curdles,
While cameras pan across the land,
Like the eyes of God mocking faulty foundations.
Hungry water keeps churning forward where it wants to go,
Insisting we learn what we don't want to know.

First Day of Spring

The first day of spring came
With snow on the ground,
Invasion in the headlines,
Determined tulip tips,
Pushing through mud.

Civilian corpses bled into packed sand,
Raked by shrapnel and aircraft rounds,
Mothers screamed, orphans rocked,
Crocuses opened, daffodil shoots arose,
Blue jays screeched, hawks soared
Turning on the wind, looking for prey
Peering through red buds of
Maples bleeding sweet sap.

The first day of spring came
With trains running on time
Down cold tracks like dusty mirrors,
Leading to the same destinations
Behind and ahead,
Changing images in time.
Friendly fire went awry as the planet tipped
Back toward the sun.

9/11 Redux

In his final moments
Those soulful eyes were startled and angry,
No turban on his head, no gun in his hand.

I silenced him at point blank,
with his wife screaming in the rubble,
Clear shots to the head and heart.

We could have taken him alive,
But we carried out the mission,
Arriving with body bags, not hand cuffs.

They cheered us in the streets,
Passions hot for revenge served cold,
Justice delivered for the perfect headline.

It's always been this way somewhere,
Eye for an eye, chopped heads by the desert highway,
Antoinette at the guillotine, picnic lynchings on the
    village square.

Knot

I want to look but not to be seen
Regarding what you want to be seen
Without being regarded.

Fish Nor Fowl

Before they cut off your fingers,
So you could no longer finger
The notes and chords of your powerful songs,

Before they hauled off your bullet riddled corpse,
Because you kept singing with bleeding hands
After they order you to stop,

Before I knew you in legend,
Heard your voice recorded forever to haunt and inspire,
You knew my traveling companions, these ladies on
        the train.

Fish nor fowl, you called them,
Nothing, neither here nor there,
The ones who refused to see,

Who saw and looked away while
Spewing sniveling remonstrations,
Castigating children in the streets,

For raising fists and voices,
Marching bravely before ranks of battle ready police,
Staring passively beside unblinking cameras.

Fish nor fowl—the world weary reporters with makeup
        covering their pimples,

Dressed in silk ties and blow dries, pearls and cynicism,
Assembled to pounce and spin on deadline for a forgetful,
     hungry audience.

Fish nor fowl—you already knew their desperation to have it
     both ways,
Ignoring babies in dumpsters, bloated bodies in desert
     borderlands,
Executive bonuses flowing like champagne in a continent
     thirsty for work.

Fish nor fowl—you knew their parched pronouncements,
     their mocking laughter,
Their savoir faire, cocky and unaware, glacial inequity flowing
     in crumbling rivers,
Raising seas of people into streets from Bahrain to Boston.

Fish nor fowl—you knew how long they held back the tide,
Clinging fiercely to the life rafts of their investments,
Clucking their tongues over your demise.

Fish nor fowl—cheering the tanks, toasting the generals,
Straightening paintings as the rumbling of a new order
Shook their walls.

In Lieu of Taxes

Siren songs fill the heavens,
Governor promises transparency,
Speaker heralds jobs,
Moguls seduce,
Unions thunder,
We must do the deal,
Must have our own vacuum,
To suck away the savings of low rollers
Who can't afford to gamble the market,
Must have a crystal palace
With bargain packages
For those who won't be
Wintering in the islands this year.

LeVeque Tower

An honest man is the noblest work of God and
An honest government is the noblest work of Man.
So says the bold brass medallion
Embedded in marble,
Emblazoned with the sun,
Surrounded by astrological signs,
Under foot in the lobby of the world's
Fifth tallest building circa 1927—
Taller than the Washington Monument
Tallest between New York and Chicago—
Founded in bedrock on the graves
Of five who gave their lives,
Building this citadel to the American Insurance Union.
Did the families of these noblest works
Receive fair recompense from the insurance lords
Whose tower still scrapes the sky,
Brightly adorning the night and proudly
Pointing the way toward heaven?

Museum

One may not touch this alabaster chessboard
Inlaid with semi-precious stones crafted by
Descendants of artisan slaves who built the Taj Mahal.

Nor may one sit on this exquisitely carved
Ivory chair decorated in pigment
Distilled from the urine of mango-fed cows.

We hold these truths to be self-evident:
That all relics of imperial glory
Are endowed with the right to preservation

Not that we should consider the lives of their creators,
But rather admire the tastes and fortunes
Of those who commissioned, owned, used, and bequeathed.

View from the Lock House

A photographer's dream of
Smokestacks and rusted trellises,
Pipes and parapets, tanks and tracks,
Hulks above the swollen river
Under a leaden sky,
Mausoleum for three consumed
In the explosion that's proving
Messy for regulators,
A liability for shareholders,
Who will never meet the widows,
Or the families of seven hundred
Soon to lose their jobs
As the operation moves south—
Cheaper to rebuild than repair.

9C

We plod through mud without getting dirty,
Butcher the meek without bloodying
Our hands, punching through glass
Without getting cut,
Sitting around our earnest table,
Dining on responsibility,
Cogs in a noble bureaucracy,
Flotsam on a current of villainous neglect,
Watching riches pour into coffers
Of greedy hands that opened the floodgates,
Spreadsheets arrayed,
Powerless except by subtraction,
We parry observations and clever propositions
To achieve the unthinkable,
Choosing among targets
For savings with deadly costs,
Minding turf and pecking orders,
Watching for cues, shuffling around,
Impressing one another,
Hiding ignorance,
Wincing over choices
About other people's suffering,
Eliminating jobs while holding our own,
Wrestling with deadlines,
Recalculating bottom lines,
Rolling our eyes, shaking fortunate heads,

We take momentary stock of the big picture,
The canvas of accumulated cuts,
The power of multiplication,
We peek into halls of screaming mirrors,
Slam close the doors,
Seek relief in gallows humor,
Agree on next steps
For our trek along the Styx,
Delicate assignments,
Clandestine strategies
To implement and mitigate.
We do our best,
Then disburse like rings on a poisoned lake,
Rippling out through corridors and phone lines,
Sharing bad news with appropriate parties,
Hanging our heads in private,
Crying at our desks.

Sludge People

We are the sludge people,
Oatmeal in our veins,
Oozing excuses for why we cannot do simple things
We do not want to do for others.
We carefully craft our calendars
To maintain order and avoid consequence.
We color within the lines.
Our crayons must be just so.
We guard our prerogatives,
Sit on our laurels, and stand for nothing,
Upholding the status quo we claim to eschew,
Strangers to vision, paragons of pomposity,
Shameless myopic parasites fumbling about
To lure all within reach to join us
In the mud of self-important irrelevance.

Different Planets

A new river is draining Greenland's glaciers.
Five Bangladeshi rivers wait to swallow millions,
On a rising ocean of tears our children's children
    have yet to cry.
The powerful among us flow and mingle,
Confident tributaries feeding into
A raging torrent of aspiration and denial,
Racing along as if oblivious,
Splashed in praise and possibilities,
Laughing carefree in swirling currents,
Carrying fellow travelers into boulders
    and perilous backwaters.
What if they could stop, look, and listen,
As we were taught before understanding our differences?
What if we could live in the same world?

Reality Check

He watched to see if I would approach
Her naked thighs, vacant eyes, cardboard sign,
Held limp under his controlling vigil,
A predator looking for his own next meal,
Oblivious to the dawning revolution,
Described with a confident smile by the visiting visionary
Inspiring aspirants from his laptop,
Eyes shining, erudition glowing like the moon on water,
Full of passion for a world we have yet to know,
A transformation yet to be defined,
A victory we can achieve because we must, somehow.

We Burn Crosses

We burn crosses.
We burn churches.
We burn righteous in our cause.
Our cups runneth over.
We scorn their vain complaining.
We revile their entitled weakness.
We too have known injustice and slamming doors,
Swallowed anger at every meal.

And now comes one to mock us,
A stain upon His name
The damned flock down before him
Traitors, sons of Cain.
Our nation besieged, destiny in peril.
Mongrels at the borders threaten our children.
Insanity reigns, but God is with us.
We obey His law.
We glorify His name.
We exalt His chosen people.
We avenge His will.
So we burn crosses.
We burn churches.

Keeping Still

A giant poster hung on our minister's wall,
Issuing a challenge in psychedelic colors and hippie font:
If you're not part of the solution,
You're part of the problem.
I digested it whole with King and Thoreau,
To learn as a grandfather,
It was a koan,
A lily with petals unfolding,
Dead skin settling as dust,
Forever requiring attention.

Duck and Cover

In my young America,
With music and marches,
Rallies and revelation,
It was easy to be righteous,
To know we were right,
Even with the answer
Blowin' in the Wind—
No duck and cover
With a world to change.

Little would we imagine three guys swilling beer
On the White House patio with cameras rolling:
The white cop and the black professor wrongly arrested
Chilling with the president, whose mild complaint
Ignited a fire storm of rebuke
From outraged Amerikkkans.

No way to duck and no place to cover
When cops sworn to serve protect their own,
When ministers turn out to be
Cool on race and keen on women,
When allies dine on each other,
One generation to the next,
When gray keeps revealing itself
In the blowing wind, and
The solution that seemed so clear
Was really a shape shifter.

I Heard Civilization Convincingly Declared Dead in 1975

They came down from rural Vermont
With calloused hands, iron grips, serious smiles,
A way of life, a world view
Shared in books and lectures,
The erstwhile socialist economist and the violinst,
New York exiles in the '30s,
Eschewing the academy for the good life,
Building in stone, working the land,
Trading in maple syrup and inspiration.

I shook their 90 and 70 year old hands and listened
Spellbound to their recitation,
How to divide the day in halves,
Balancing bread labor and leisure pursuits,
How civilization had died when we
Obliterated Hiroshima with the atom bomb,
How we might save ourselves, or not.

A crazy friend once said
About some milk in his mustache,
In a hundred years, who will know?
So it goes, says the novelist.
Art is mortal, says the poet.
Come to bed, says the lover,
Keeping me ever hopeful.

How I Saved My Cousin From
A Life of Infamy

My mother says my cousin blames me
For being denied CIA employment.
Who knew when I wrote that letter to Nixon,
Quoting Masters of War,
Bringing a Secret Service agent to my door,
When we marched, with the Red Squad
Clinging to street light poles, heaving heavy cameras,
When we swallowed tear gas on the Capitol lawn,
Sang Handel from a city jail cell,
Who knew the fate from which my cousin escaped,
If it's true, what my mother said.

Something Else the Gipper Got Wrong

Ronald Reagan said there's
Nothing better for the inside of a man
Than the outside of a horse.
Obviously not a swimmer.

Waves

Bella Figura

We come naked before you,
Sailing and writing,
Bodies flowing like notes,
But this is not jazz.
We know exactly where we will land.

My hand on her shoulder,
Her thigh in my hand,
We should make love like this,
With impossible extension of exquisite limbs.

Cauldrons of fire illuminate the stage,
Curtains constrain space and time,
We move in dreams,
Testing the limits of tension,
Offering ourselves, correcting, relaxing.

We stride from the wings,
Emerge from the womb,
Leap, run, and find our places,
Flames and shadows in each other's arms.

The Band

We live this way
Time travelers layering
The sweet legato
Sharp staccato
Rapid ostinato
Stitching ourselves
Into the plan, the flow,
Here we go, smiling
Finding the way together
Always in the ever-changing
Groove, on the move,
Coming to your town
Tomorrow and yesterday
We live this way,
Time travelers,
We play.

Tip Top

I like this place, the Tip Top,
Formerly the Vine, with its
Rock music and shaggy sideburns,
Dangling earrings and thick rimmed glasses,
Grime on aprons,
Bistro grub on plate,
Columbus Pale Ale, Ohio State,
Steel studded belts and frilly lace blouses,
Blond trusses, tight jeans,
High boots and lip rings.
It's my music, too, you know,
The pulsing bass and sweet guitars.
I look older than I feel,
Feel older than I look,
Look and look away
As you carry drinks and breasts
Back and forth with your tray.
I admire the molded tin ceiling
With old paint peeling,
The crystal and brass chandeliers
With dusty, red velvet chain covers
Anchored in history.
Listen,
These walls have stories to tell.
The bricks are watching.
The crystals shimmer and shake
To the new beat that never changes—

My past your future,
My future so fast,
Our time so fleeting,
Our hearts all beating, so slow,
It's a nice place you've got here,
A nice life we all share
So briefly, so sorry
It's time to go.

Pelican

Only death could still his pen,
Neither critics, nor self-doubt scurrying crab-like
Among the slime covered rocks of his formative years,
Adulation of future generations beside the point.

He wrote ferociously, driven
By demons, observations, positions
Catching and refracting the light like earrings
Dangling on the lovely shaved head of her potential.

He was determined that reason and irony
Might shame warmongers into contrition,
Illuminating incessant dark capacities
Festering and blooming in every age.

Likewise, she dives, a pelican
Plucking sustenance from the cool green depths of hope,
Spitting out bitter salt water to consume
Each hard won morsel of daring,

Bill tucked in as if piercing her own breast,
The very symbol of fecund devotion,
She rises on graceful wings, taking up the paintbrush,
Exposing pieces of herself, frame by frame,

Vulnerable to casual judgment and capricious indifference,
Growing despite all odds
In rocky crevices and sun bleached sand,
Persevering, reworking each image,

Perfecting her craft, editing and polishing,
Balancing on the razor edges
Of every facet, aware of the inclusions,
Driven to shine.

Constellation

You thanked me
For seeing you through your work,
Hoped I'd find inspiration.
Well, it was inspiration like reading Whitman
When my acne was fresh.
So thank you for sharing
Your life wide open, your mastery,
And I have to ask,
When don't you shimmer and
Did you know the Incas
Saw constellations not in the stars
But in the dark places between?

Eat That Chicken

You pull on a weathered jersey,
Navy blue over crimson camisole,
Carelessly covering coveted breasts,
Then fix me with your smiling eyes and say,
So now you know what's underneath.
Oh Lawd, I want to eat that chicken.

You speak out from your poet's grave,
Black words printed on brown faded pages,
The soul of dignity remembering a lilac dusk—
Hydrangeas beckoned from outside your prison window
As you thought of leaving your lover at dawn.
Oh Lawd, I want to eat that chicken.

You pluck the strings and hold the beat,
Blue notes dancing in a storm of joy,
Africa in your bones as you play the rhythm
Of freedom seized from Jim Crow's cauldron,
Time wizard carrying us high beyond our fears, singing,
Oh Lawd, I want to eat that chicken.

Transported

I can hear your voice
Reading these poems

Hear uncomposed music
Behind these lyrics

Hear survivors' laments
Rise in your verse

See them facing an altar
Intoning your words

Embrace their hope
Carry their pain

Feel sweltering sun,
Smell cooling rain

Hear family and friends
Sing amen, amen, amen

In these poems, your poems
I read from the page.

We Carry On

Only the songs and the poems remain
Bittersweet fragments of dreams,
You gave us your best and then you surrendered.
Now we carry on.

Dangling alone like a song out of time,
Deaf to the rhythms of change,
Estranged from your muse and hope's sweet inspiration,
That we carry on.

I live with anger and love for you still,
Learning the pulse of your strum,
Missing the light you gave in dark hours,
And still carry on.

We carry on from the roots you once nourished
We carry on with the work you laid down,
We carry on with proud new generations,
Yes, we carry on.

This is What Democracy Looks Like

Ashes spew from your mouth, your eyes, your wherever.
Poisonous truths revealed in transparent lies
Erupt from your unchecked need and unbound greed.
But we are now accustomed to your seething fulminations.
We share a different vision for our fragmented nation.
We sing together on subway cars,
Chant shoulder-to-shoulder in the streets,
Share hope and heart and humor
Across race and age and gender.
We find courage in our numbers,
Love in the eyes of strangers,
Crevices of possibility in the crust of your inhumanity.
We rise and resist despite the risk.
We listen and learn,
Standing on shoulders,
Finding the way forward as we take our turn.

Election Victory

Poems are springing out of thin air!
People can't help themselves
From speaking in stanzas.
Something has come unloose, unshackled.
You said it:
Hope is a wonderful thing,
Perhaps the most important thing.

Midterm Fears

I rose early to see the full eclipse,
But Luna had already slipped out the Western exit.
Maybe she left with Veritas and Themis
To lick her wounds, bloodied as she was
By the shadows of the orange one's
Legions flooding the eastern sky
Amber growing ever brighter,
A pyre of books burning under the horizon,
A lake of fire, the second ring,
A bell about to toll.
Maybe they retreated together
With the ghosts of those for whom we march,
Holding in their determined arms
Dreams of migrants lost at sea.
Maybe they went singing in the tongues of families
Perished in deserts, of nations lost in floods,
Knowing their time will come
With new generations arriving
To claim the night and carry the day.

Proposition 8

It was poison they were drinking,
Nonsense they were thinking,
Holding back the tide.

Seeds lie fallow for a reason,
To flourish in their season,
Breaking stone in stride.

Mountains rise through land once covered by the sea,
As love demands unbounded liberty,
With dignity and pride.

Ailanthus

On the winter solstice,
We made them drag us away,
The longest night,
The shortest day.

Now the sun comes into its own,
The source of life shines longer,
Darkness shrinks from the justice we have done,
And our wills grown stronger.

With a full moon smiling,
You come to share your dreams—
Communion table and
Prison scenes.

Now the gates are open to the Word,
The oceans swell in glory,
Hands are set to the work that must be done,
The finest human story.

So let the sun and the moon
Set the tune.

Why We Do It

Because we have something to say,
Want to be noticed, like to have fun, enjoy the applause
Walking, strutting, striding to the mike
To the heady beat of music.

Because we like to listen,
Remember, imagine
Live in each other's lives
See with each other's eyes.

Because we need to create,
Relate, forsake
Force fed platitudes
And attitudes.

Because we delight in surprises
Sudden bursts of beauty
Wit and wisdom
From old friends and total strangers.

Because of the colors
Refracted in these black walls
The open skies in this closed space
The world on these benches.

Because, briefly spinning about the sun,
We have something to say.

Bioluminescent Bay

We undulate and twirl,
Spreading star streams with every touch,
Flying through liquid space,
Lights out, breaths suspended,
Dolphin souls dreaming,
Laughing silently, amazed.
Couldn't this last forever, please,
This generous, twinkling love?

Behind the Green Glass Door

Behind the green glass door, you can find
Screaming parrots in black trees,
Robbed by cunning eagles,
Empanadillas with cheese, tossed in paper towels,
Freedom in yearning murals, painted the colors of anger
    and hope,
Struggle each day for our daily bread,
Needles and pee in one way streets,
Dresses of yellow and green,
Parrot colors, a queer sound rising,
A deep stirring song,
Passion, pride overflowing,
A waterfall that can't be stopped.
Behind the green glass door,
Bankers stutter, brokers shudder,
Students see what the professors miss,
The moon rises through coral clouds,
The ocean swells, alive with light.

The Winds of El Morro

Kites litter the cliffs of El Morro, hanging from trees facing
    the sea.
Children's dreams soared on the wind but were dashed here,
Falling to rest where feral cats wander and
Strings dangle from foreboding walls,
Built for conquistadors by enslaved Tainos.

Vejigante dances here. Iguana roams. Coqui sings.
Courage courses through Borinquen veins.
Girls stand between their mothers and knife wielding men.
Abuelas break locks and chains
To occupy schools and cook for bedridden neighbors.

Evening light is soft on the cliffs of El Morro.
Shadows lengthen. Warm waters whisper of howling winds
    and the uncounted dead.
The governor raises his glass in La Fortaleza,
Concerned only with the needs of his puppeteer,
An ash on the wind, a bitter taste on history's tongue.

Butterflies dance among flamboyant trees,
Mariposa, symbol of transformation, of all things possible:
Solidarity after chaos, the power of community,
The one who conquers fear,
The loving gaze, the nod, the decision to continue.

The winds of El Morro carry kites through curtains of heat,
Up toward the sun who pours sweat on the brow of
    the gardener,
The security guard, the fruit seller, the housekeeper,
The bridge builder, the dancers, smooth as flan,
And children with hands proudly on the strings, dreams
    ever soaring.

We Who Believe

Save us from precious
Do this, do that poems,
Holier than thou directives on
How to breathe the sunlight,
Drink the stardust,
Be the ripe tomato.
I want to be one in the number,
Listening, learning,
Love in action,
Chisels and knives sharp
Until the end.

Winter Solstice

I should be sleeping, though at this hour,
My grandfather would have been hard at work,
Delivering milk in the dark Minnesota winter,
Silver light of the setting moon bathing vacant streets
With the glow of memory, hard truths, distant dreams,
Awaiting dawn's flood of pumpkin, mustard, and coral,
Glad for the sun to begin its shortest arc of the year.

At the dinner table, he blew air into his thumb,
Inflating his biceps as we laughed and pleaded, do it again,
Grandmom smiling as he continued, teasing into forever,
Where they live now, out of touch after all these years,
Inhabiting the realm of gratitude, longing, and regret,
Denizens of dreams, from which I wake to find you.

I marvel at the distance between us,
How long we have been out of touch,
Remembering work that brought us together,
Comings and goings through the years,
Our orbits and elliptical paths,
Across chasms of time and space.

So many journeys side by side,
Rolling up our sleeves to get the jobs done,
Tasks, missions, struggles,
Achievements of lifetimes,

Transformations now celebrated or forgotten
As new generations claim the day.

I wonder at my ignorance about particle physics,
Monarch migrations, schooling fishes,
Gravity and changing currents of ocean and air,
How the giant upon whose shoulders we stand
Stoops under the weight of years,
How acorns and pinecones settle and grow,

How one may calculate the precise moment
When earth's axis tilts furthest from the sun,
Turning at the edge of hope,
As memory releases the dead and love propels the living
To reach out, to honor and praise, to say thank you,
I miss you, hoping our orbits intersect again,
Before we join the remembered ones.

For My Students

I would tell you
Love and justice are inseparable,
Change usually comes too slowly.

I am still learning, striving like you
To understand and make my place.
The gap of a generation

Is like a meteor tail,
A beaver slap on water,
Less than the blink of a wary eye.

I would say our choices matter,
Pay attention to lichen
Gently eating rock and making way for forests.

Beware those who encourage dismissive judgement,
Who would fashion you in their own image,
Who believe they have the answers

To questions you must answer
With loving work, relation and creation
Over time, in community, on your own.

Notes on Selected Poems

Quabbin (p. 15) refers to the Quabbin Reservoir, largest fresh water body of water in Massachusetts, built in the 1930s by damming the Swift River and submerging four towns to provide drinking water for Boston and other communities. Quabbin derives from the Nipmuc (Native American) word for "place of many waters."

Water is Body (p. 24) flows from Natalie Diaz's, "The First Water is the Body," in *Postcolonial Love Poem* (Minneapolis: Graywolf Press, 2020), p. 46. Credit also to a line in Herman Hesse's *Siddhartha*, "Time is not real, Govinda," (New York: New Directions, 1951), p. 115. And to A.J. Juarez for the observation, "Death is for the living."

If It Bleeds (p. 49) was inspired by a story with photograph in the *Boston Globe*, "Storm Brings Haiti More Misery" November 6, 2010, p. 1.

In *Fires in the West* (p. 66), the lines, "...beauty is the splendor of truth," and "Beautiful that the apprehension of which pleases..." are quotes from Plato and Aquinas, respectively, in James Joyce, *Portrait of the Artist as a Young Man* (New York: Viking, 1956), p. 208 and p.207.

Fish Nor Fowl (p. 72) is for Victor Jara and derives its title from his song of that name.

9C (p. 78) refers to a section of Massachusetts law that authorizes the governor to impose cuts to certain areas of the state budget without legislative approval in case of a projected revenue deficit.

We Burn Crosses (p. 83) was inspired by the firebombing of Macedonia Church of God in Christ in Springfield, MA hours after Barak Obama's 2008 election as U.S. president.

Keeping Still (p. 84) derives its title from the poem by Pablo Neruda, "Keeping Quiet."

I Heard Civilization Convincingly Declared Dead in 1975 (p. 86) refers to Helen and Scott Nearing.

Bella Figura (p. 91) was inspired by the ballet of that name by Jiří Kylián.

Pelican (p. 95) is for the artist Sara Risley, with reference also to Kurt Vonnegut Jr.

Constellation (p. 97) was written for Porsha Olayiwola.

Eat That Chicken (p. 98) is in appreciation of Dennis Brutus and Charles Mingus.

Transported (p. 99) is in reaction to "Faith" by Kwame Dawes.

We Carry On (p. 100) is for Phil Ochs.

Proposition 8 (p. 104) was in reaction to the 2008 California ballot initiative and constitutional amendment to ban same-sex marriage.

We Who Believe (p. 111) takes inspiration from Ella Baker, with appreciation to Barbara Ransby for her biography of Baker and to Bernice Johnson Reagon for "Ella's Song."

Acknowledgements

Too many people inspired these poems from too many spheres over too long a time to attempt a full listing. They include family and friends, organizers, activists, community leaders, artists in all forms, clergy, teachers, mentors, students, and work colleagues with diverse worldviews. Suffice to say I am indebted to an incredible community of people with whom I have been fortunate to share this life, and from whom I continue to learn.

Special thanks to A.J. Juarez, who invited this manuscript and who has been a tremendous support throughout its preparation, particularly in sharing wisdom about creativity, courage, and the artistic process. I would not have done this without his encouragement. His painting graces the cover and beautifully embraces the book's themes.

Thank you also to Julie Murkette, Publisher of Satya House Publications, for her vision and determination, and to Sarah Bennett, whose graphic design, editing, and production skills transformed an email attachment into the book you now hold.

Thank you to my parents, Norman Wilkinson and Diana March, for their love and for the values they passed to and through my sisters and me. Thank you to my sons, Dan and Steve, and to their loves, Nicole and Molly. Thank you to our grandchildren, Max and Evelyn, with hope they will find inspiration here. Thank you, reader, for listening and imagining.

Mostly, thank you to my beloved and closest friend, Sally Johnson, who inspired many of these poems, read or listened to all of them, and helped select those that appear in these pages. Our meeting was the confluence that has most shaped my life.

About the Author

Geoff Wilkinson is a professor at Boston University School of Social Work, where he teaches community organizing, advocacy, and organizational change. A lifelong activist, he worked as a community organizer and as executive director of two statewide organizations advancing health, housing, and social justice, the Massachusetts Senior Action Council and the Massachusetts Public Health Association. He also served as senior policy advisor to the commissioner and director of policy and planning for the Massachusetts Department of Public Health. Wilkinson is a founding board member and treasurer of the National Association of Community Health Workers. He is also a co-founder of two organizations working to promote peace and affordable housing, respectively, in the town where he lives just south of Boston with his wife of over 40 years. They have two married sons and two grandchildren. This is his first book.

CPSIA information can be obtained
at www.ICGtesting.com
Printed in the USA
LVHW041942280423
745612LV00019B/263